Detroit's Historic Hotels and Restaurants

Bird's-Eye view of Campus, Detroit, Mich.

The Campus Martius, also called Cadillac Square, was the center of the business district and was near many of Detroit's hotels and restaurants. The Campus Martius was where the Detroit Opera House was located and was the end of the line for the railway and electric street cars. The Soldiers and Sailors Monument in the foreground commemorates the lives of the 14,823 Michigan servicemen who died in the Civil War.

On the front cover: Please see page 13. (Author's collection.)

On the back cover: Please see page 81. (Author's collection.)

POSTCARD HISTORY SERIES

Detroit's Historic Hotels and Restaurants

Patricia Ibbotson

ARCADIA
PUBLISHING

Published by Arcadia Publishing
Charleston SC, Chicago IL, Portsmouth NH, San Francisco CA

Printed in the United States of America

Library of Congress Catalog Card Number: 2007924628

For all general information contact Arcadia Publishing at:
Telephone 843-853-2070
Fax 843-853-0044
E-mail sales@arcadiapublishing.com
For customer service and orders:
Toll-Free 1-888-313-2665

Visit us on the Internet at www.arcadiapublishing.com

Speramus Meliora; Resurget Cineribus
We Hope for Better Things; It Shall Rise from the Ashes
The motto of the City of Detroit

CONTENTS

ACKNOWLEDGMENTS

My special thanks are due to the following people who have contributed in some way to my ability to gather materials and information for this book: Bertha M. Miga, archives staff, Dearborn Historical Museum, McFadden Ross House; Melanie Bazil, senior archivist, Henry Ford Health Services, Archives and Historical Collection; Debbie Larsen, Mount Clemens Public Library; Elizabeth Kelley Kerstens, archivist, Plymouth Historical Society; Donna Garbarino, adult services librarian, Troy Public Library; Michael Fish, archivist, Municipal Archives, Windsor Public Library, Windsor, Ontario, Canada; Phyllis Evans of Redford, whose grandparents ran the Paradiso Café; Roma Café for a postcard of the restaurant; Karl Kurz for a postcard of the Dakota Inn Rathskeller; and Charlie Hyde, professor of history, Wayne State University, for sharing his memories of Webster Hall.

INTRODUCTION

Detroit grew at a phenomenal rate starting at the dawn of the 20th century and reaching its peak in the 1950s. The biggest boom era was the period between 1915 and 1927 when people and businesses poured into the city. By the 1920s, Detroit was the fourth largest city in the United States. With this growth, many visitors came to the city for business or pleasure or a combination of both.

The city was also home to many conventions, with the annual Detroit Automobile Show being one of the first. The Detroit Automobile Show celebrated its 100th anniversary in 2007. In 1910, this show was held at the Wayne Gardens of the Wayne Hotel and Pavilion, and by then it was already a major event. The automobile show was only one of many big conventions in Detroit. Around 1925, the National Association of Real Estate Boards held a convention with more than 1,000 people in attendance. Other conventions of that time period included the National Association of Piano Tuners, the Heating and Piping Contractors, and the Ice Cream Manufacturer's. The Brotherhood of Locomotive Firemen and Engineers held a convention in Detroit that lasted 30 days. Grindley's Convention Hall, built in 1924, was then the largest exhibition hall in the United States and was 10 minutes away from all the major hotels. All the Detroit Automobile Shows were held at Grindley's Convention Hall until World War II. Cobo Hall is the current conference and exhibition center. It opened in 1960 and was named after Albert E. Cobo, who was mayor of Detroit from 1950 through 1957.

Thousands of people passed through Detroit by train whose railroad tickets allowed for a 10-day stopover, so many used it as an opportunity to visit the city. One thing that made Detroit so popular with visitors is that it had so many activities available, such as river riding on the D&W (Detroit and Windsor) ferries, visiting Belle Isle, Put-in-Bay, the Flats, Mount Clemens, Sugar Island, Bob-Lo, and Tashmoo Park. The proximity of Detroit to Windsor and Amherstburg, Ontario, Canada, was another drawing card.

Whether traveling for business or pleasure, visitors could also avail themselves to live theater, ballets, and symphonies at the Shubert, Cass, Fox, and the Detroit Masonic Temple. There were also several grand movie theaters—the Adams, United Artists, Madison, the Fisher (now a live theater)—in the downtown area. The Detroit Opera House was also popular with visitors as was Olympia Stadium, where there was ice hockey, ice shows, basketball, and big concerts. Visitors were also drawn to sporting events such as baseball and football games.

There were 75 hotels listed in the 1890 Detroit city directory. Many of the early hotels had French names reflecting Detroit's early French culture. There was the Ste. Claire Hotel, the Cadillac Hotel, the Hotel Normandie, and the Pontchartrain.

During 1924 and 1925, Detroit saw the opening of 20 new hotels in an 18-month period. The biggest were the Book Cadillac and Webster Hall. The Book Cadillac is currently being renovated into a hotel and condominium complex. Webster Hall has been torn down. The others, which are all gone now, were the Alartley, Carleton-Plaza, Emerson, Eddystone, Edison, Fairbairn, Gotham, Lewis, Lexington, Martha Washington, Mount Royal, Palmetto, Paul Revere, Park Avenue Roosevelt, Royal Palm, Stratford Arms, Washington, plus other smaller hotels. By 1937, Detroit had about 10 million visitors a year and had over 200 hotels with approximately 25,000 guest rooms. One can find a lot of history in the architecture of the old hotels. If their walls could speak, what tales they could tell.

In 1937, William M. Walker, the president of the Detroit Hotel Association and trustee managing director of the Hotel Fort Shelby was interviewed for a radio talk program, and he said that the Hotel Fort Shelby used 600,000 little cakes of soap, 360,000 face towels, and 10,000 bath towels a year as well as 15,000 gallons of ink, which were used to pen those "wish you were here" postcards. The messages written on the hotel postcards give insight into the traveler's thoughts at the time. Many were written just to let family or friends know they arrived safely or to inform them of their itinerary.

The many restaurants of Detroit provided food and entertainment for residents and visitors. They ranged from the self-serve, cafeteria-style to the elegant, with many ethnic restaurants reflecting Detroit's cultural diversity. Most of these restaurants are gone now, too, replaced by the chain restaurants one sees all around the world.

Many hotels and restaurants gave out or mailed postcards as advertising. Guests could find them at the registration desk in a hotel or at the cashier in a restaurant. Some hotels and restaurants would even supply the postage. Krager's German restaurant on Gratiot Avenue had a message on the postcard that said "We will gladly affix stamp. Address and hand to server."

By the 1960s, tourists were lured to the new motels in the suburbs as travel by automobile increased while train travel decreased dramatically. After the riots of the late 1960s, downtown business plummeted. Now Detroit is in a renaissance, and new businesses, housing, and hotels are springing up. Detroit is starting to awaken to its own history. The old Barlum Hotel was recently converted into the New Cadillac Gardens apartments. The Book Cadillac is being refurbished into the new Westin Book Cadillac, which will have 455 hotel rooms, 67 condominiums on the upper floors, restaurants, retail space, and a conference center. There are also plans to renovate the Fort Shelby hotel into a 204-room Doubletree Guest Suites hotel. It will include 63 apartments and about 30,000 square feet of convention space.

Detroit's Historic Hotels and Restaurants includes nearly 50 hotels and over 40 restaurants from Detroit in the first two chapters and others from the Detroit metropolitan area in the third chapter. Almost all of the postcards are from the author's private collection. Most of the information on the hotels and restaurants was gleaned from the back of the postcards, old newspaper clippings, the Detroit and Dearborn city directories, the reading room files in the Burton Historical Collection of the Detroit Public Library, and the Internet.

One

DETROIT'S HOTELS

While it would have been ideal to be able to include a postcard of every early hotel in Detroit, it was not possible to do so in terms of both the numbers of hotels and the availability of postcards. Most of the largest and better known hotels have been included—the Tuller, the Pontchartrain, the Statler, the Book Cadillac, the Detroit Leland, the Webster, and the Whittier—as well as some smaller, lesser known hotels including the Andoria, the North Pole, and the Yorba. The earliest hotel included is the Russell House, which opened in 1857. There were only about 50 hotels listed in the 1862 Detroit city directory. The proprietor of the Russell House in 1862 was L. T. Minor. Some postcards of the hotel dining rooms and restaurants are included as well as some great interior views of these vintage hotels. There are also several postcards of early Detroit motels. A few of these motels are still in business. Two hotels in Highland Park have been included with the Detroit postcards because Highland Park was and still is a small city almost completely surrounded by Detroit. The population of Highland Park shot up after Henry Ford opened his Highland Park Ford Plant there in 1910.

CADILLAC SQUARE, DETROIT, MICH.

9-11-07.

On the right is the Russell House, which was one of Detroit's most famous hotels. The Russell House was the old National Hotel, which had been built in 1836. It became the Russell House in 1857. Additions were put on in 1875 and 1876, and the center of the building was reconstructed in 1881. Asa Henry signed his name and wrote the date 9–11–07 on the front of this card, which was postmarked the same day. He sent this card to William Roberson in Buffalo, New York. This popular hotel was the site of many weddings and social events. Famous guests included the Prince of Wales and Mark Twain. The lawn across the bottom of the postcard was in front of the city hall. The building in the center back is the Wayne County Building, which was built in 1902, has since been restored, and is still being used for county offices.

G 3823a. St Claire Hotel, Detroit, Mich.

The Ste. Clair Hotel was built in 1879 by William G. Thompson, a mayor of Detroit. A later owner was James D. Burns who previously owned the Detroit Baseball Club and had been the Wayne County sheriff for four years. Burns built the Burns Hotel in 1905, sold his interest to his partner in 1915, and bought the Ste. Clair Hotel. John R. Stirling and Sons were the proprietors in the 1920s when the street address was 305 Monroe Avenue. The hotel was a swanky showplace with 110 guest rooms. It billed itself as completely fireproof, and the rooms had a view of city hall and the Soldiers and Sailors Monument on the Campus Martius. It was conveniently located in the civic center near businesses, restaurants, and the theaters. It was torn down in 1934.

The Wayne Hotel and Pavilion was built in 1885 on the site of the old Cass Hotel at Jefferson Avenue and Third Street. It was Detroit's most popular hotel as it was situated right across the street from the Michigan Central Railroad Station and fronted on the Detroit River. It had cascading fountains, marble floors, deep carpets, and glittering chandeliers. The proprietor was James R. Hayes who had a walrus mustache and a genial disposition.

In another view of the Wayne Hotel and Pavilion, looking east from Broadway Street, one can see the horse-drawn carriages and the other businesses, including a wines and spirits shop, that once lined Jefferson Avenue. Hotel guests did not have to go far for wines and spirits as the hotel had three bars. It also had five dining rooms where, on Sunday, a special dinner was served for $1.

D. & C. Dock, Wayne Hotel and New Bath House,
Detroit, Mich.

This postcard, postmarked in 1917 and mailed from Windsor, Ontario, Canada, shows the Wayne Hotel and Pavilion from the Detroit River. The early automobile shows were held in the Wayne Gardens. The roof of the Wayne Gardens became popular as a convention auditorium. The upper story of the Wayne Gardens housed a restaurant where one could dine overlooking the Detroit River. The Wayne Gardens were connected to the hotel by an enclosed runway from the second story across Front Street. The hotel also was connected to a mineral bathhouse that featured hydrotherapeutic treatments. Included in the hotel complex was the Detroit and Cleveland Lane Lines. Ships left from here for Mackinac, Buffalo, Cleveland, and Toledo. Every other ferry for Belle Isle also landed here. Back in those days one could make a round trip from Belle Isle, with stops at Third Street, Woodward Avenue, and Joseph Campau Avenue, all day on a single ticket priced at 10¢.

Wayne Hotel and Pavilion, Detroit, Mich.

Another view of the Wayne Hotel and Pavilion shows the riverfront and a docked passenger ship. The hotel had a pavilion built out to the water's edge. This hotel was called a "haven for honeymooners" as so many couples from all over Michigan spent their honeymoons there. Business fell off after the new train station was built on Fifteenth Street in 1914. The building was razed in 1931.

Daniel Scotten built the Cadillac Hotel in April 1888. Scotten came to Detroit from New York and established a tobacco company in 1856 that made him very wealthy. He invested heavily in Detroit and Canadian real estate. The hotel was named after Antoine Laumet, sieur de Lamothe Cadillac, the founder of the city of Detroit.

14

In another postcard of the Cadillac Hotel postmarked August 2, 1906, one can see how the hotel was situated and how Washington Boulevard looked at the time. The hotel was at Michigan Avenue and Washington Boulevard. It was torn down in 1923 and is now the site of the Book Cadillac Hotel. This postcard was sent to Elizebeth Penzer at the Fountain Hotel in Yellowstone Park, Wyoming.

This is the Cadillac Hotel on a postcard postmarked 1912 and sent to Mrs. A. W. Davis of Grass Lake. This was the third hotel to occupy this site. The first was built by Nathaniel Champe who later leased it to a firm who operated it as the Temperance House. The second was built by John Blindbury who operated it for 15 years; then it was leased and called the Antisdel.

Hotel Normandie. Detroit, Mich.

The Hotel Normandie opened in April 1890. It was situated on Congress Street East, a half block from Woodward Avenue. It had 125 rooms with steam heat and electricity supplied by its own plant. The proprietors in 1896 were Francis H. Carr and Edgar F. Reeves. The restaurant meals were the feature of the hotel and they cost 50¢ each.

Another early Detroit hotel was the Hotel Morgan, which was built around 1898. It had 110 rooms and was located at the corner of Cass Avenue and Bagley Street. It advertised as being "in the center of everything." By 1920, the hotel had been remodeled and refurnished and was owned by Frank T. Merrill.

New Tuller Hotel, Detroit, Mich.

219696

This undated postcard is titled the New Tuller Hotel, perhaps referring to the later boxy addition. There are still many postcards available of the Hotel Tuller, which was built in 1906 as a nine-floor hotel and had four additional stories added by 1914; it was expanded again in 1923 and 1929. The hotel originally had 600 rooms, but was expanded to 800. The hotel was located on Grand Circus Park bounded by Adams Avenue West, Bagley Street, and Park Avenue. The proprietor was Lewis W. Tuller, and it was one of three hotels he built in Detroit. The hotel was beautiful inside, and the ground floor rooms were joined by a wood-paneled Peacock Alley named after a space in New York's Waldorf Astoria. There was the Rose Room that served afternoon tea and the Cascade Room that offered a waterfall fountain along with a cabaret. There was also a large ballroom and four conference rooms. Later a grill room was added in the basement. The hotel was known as the "grande dame of Grand Circus Park" during the 1920s.

This postcard of the Hotel Tuller was postmarked in 1911. It was mailed as an advertisement to the Young Fuel and Pure Ice Company in Battle Creek. The message was typed as follows: "When touring to Detroit please remember that we are headquarters for touring parties. Garage directly across the road. Our reasonable rates of $1.50 per day and up should attract you for room and bath in this beautifully situated hostelry. Three blocks from center of the business district. Grand Roof Garden and Crystal Grill. Yours truly, HOTEL TULLER." At the time the hotel was competing for business with the Pontchartrain as well as some smaller hotels. The beautiful, graceful curved architecture of the original hotel can be clearly seen on this rare postcard.

The postmark cannot be read on this pre-1914 postcard of the Hotel Tuller and Grand Circus Park. The church next to the hotel was the Church of Our Father, a Universalist church, which was built in 1881 and was located at Macomb Street and Park Avenue. At the time, there were wide-open spaces on Grand Circus Park.

The wide open spaces around Hotel Tuller can be seen on this undated color postcard. Some people thought Lewis W. Tuller was crazy when he built his hotel so far out from what was then the center of the city. From left to right are the Michigan Conservatory of Music, Church of Our Father, Hotel Tuller, the Charlevoix Apartments, and the Fine Arts Building.

This view of the Hotel Tuller was taken from Grand Circus Park. The postcard is dated August 11, 1910, and bears a postmark of the same year. Rates then were $1.50 a day and up for a single room with a bath and $2.50 for a double room with a bath. Hotel guests could sit on a park bench and enjoy the shade from the trees and a view of the fountain.

Here is another view of the Hotel Tuller on a postcard postmarked 1915 that shows the addition from 1914. It was sent to a Mrs. M. Moblo in Peoria, Illinois, from a woman who signed her name Bertha and said "all are well and happy." Detroit was a growing city, and the area around the hotel was beginning to become built up.

LOBBY, HOTEL TULLER, DETROIT, MICH.

The grand lobby of the Hotel Tuller complete with crystal chandeliers, potted plants, and quality furnishings of the time is shown here in a postcard postmarked 1916. There was a writing room beyond the lobby that was decorated in blues and creams where visitors to Detroit could write postcards and letters home.

Main Arabian Restaurant, Hotel Tuller, Detroit, Mich.

The main, elegant wood-paneled Arabian restaurant of the Hotel Tuller is shown here in an undated postcard. When the hotel was extensively modernized in the art moderne style in 1943, much of the original style of the hotel was lost except for this room. The grand ballroom featured the best of the big bands. The hotel band was Pete Bontsema and his orchestra in the 1920s.

INDOOR ROOF GARDEN, HOTEL TULLER, DETROIT, MICHIGAN
A DELIGHTFUL PLACE TO DINE ON A SUMMER'S EVE

We didn't find this ones but are just as nice. D.A.R convention today but none of our family here

The Hotel Tuller also had an indoor roof garden that was "a delightful place to dine on a summer's eve." In the days before central air conditioning, a roof garden would have been the ideal place to eat in the summer; perhaps the diners could even catch a cool breeze from the Detroit River. This postcard was postmarked in 1911.

HOTEL TULLER, DETROIT, MICH.,
800 Rooms   800 Baths
Three Distinctive Restaurants

This postcard of the Hotel Tuller is dated September 15, 1926, and when referring to the hotel, the sender wrote, "how grand it is." By the mid-1920s, the Tuller had a hard time competing with the Book Cadillac and the Statler. It went through bankruptcy in the 1930s and became part of the Albert Pick chain that later also operated the Hotel Fort Shelby.

This color postcard features Grand Circus Park with the Edison Memorial Fountain in the center. The fountain was named for the inventor Thomas Alva Edison and was a focal point of the park close to Hotel Tuller, which can be seen in the background. The fountain was dedicated on October 21, 1929, and Edison and Pres. Herbert Hoover attended the dedication ceremony.

The lovely Hotel Tuller with its new addition is shown again on this color postcard from the 1920s. This postcard was published by the United News Company of Detroit.

Hotel Tuller, Detroit, Michigan

From a grand beginning, the Hotel Tuller, shown here at its peak with Grand Circus Park in the foreground, faded into a shabby residential hotel that was eventually torn down in 1976 and turned into a gravel parking lot. The 300 residents, most of them elderly, were given only eight days to find alternative accommodations.

Burns Hotel, Cadillac Square, Detroit, Mich.

BURNS HOTEL

The Burns Hotel opened in 1905 and was located on Cadillac Square and Bates Street. It was owned by James D. Burns and James A. Singelyn. Singelyn was an officer of the old Tivoli Brewing Company and undersheriff of Wayne County. He bought out Burns in 1915. The hotel was torn down to make way for the Barlum Hotel, which was built on the same site in 1927.

THE HOTEL PONTCHARTRAIN DETROIT. MICH

Another famous, elegant Detroit hotel was the Pontchartrain, which opened in October 1907. The managers were George H. Woolley and William J. Chittenden. They allowed guests to take the coffee spoons that bore the engraved crest of the hotel and a likeness of the hotel as souvenirs of the grand opening. All the hotel glassware was from L. B. King and Company and all had the Pontchartrain crest. The hotel's kitchen had 14 Jewel hotel ranges made by the Detroit Stove Works, and it also had a branch of the Schetter Drug Store off the main lobby for the convenience of the guests. This card, postmarked 1909, shows the hotel in its original form with only 10 stories. Referring to the hotel's saloon, the sender wrote that "this place has one of the finest 'cold tea' rooms in the world." Seven presidents were said to have taken refreshments at the hotel's famous mahogany bar, which was 32 feet long and 28 inches wide. Whisky was two drinks for a quarter and beer was a nickel a glass.

This hotel was built on the site of the old Russell House that had closed in 1905. It was designed by George Mason who later designed the Detroit Masonic Temple. The "Pontch," as it was nicknamed, was the gathering place for all the Detroit automobile pioneers.

The Pontchartrain is shown in a slightly different view in this postcard postmarked 1917. The original fort at Detroit was called Fort Pontchartrain after the French marine minister Jérôme de Phélypeaux, comte de Pontchartrain who never set foot in Detroit, but had both a fort and a hotel named after him. His portrait hung in the hotel saloon.

The Flamingo Room of the Pontchartrain is shown on this undated postcard. The carpet was green and the walls were deep red with the mural of pink flamingos in the arch in the center. The pillars were gold at the top as was the arch. All the furnishings were the newest and the best of the times.

Hotel Pontchartrain, Detroit, Mich.

Here is a fourth view of the Pontchartrain, which eventually had 15 stories above ground and three stories underground. Over five million pounds of steel were used in its construction. Five more stories were added to the top in 1916 in an effort to compete with the new Statler hotel. It was situated on the southeast corner of Cadillac Square and billed itself as modern and fireproof with reasonable rates.

Here again is the Pontchartrain with a view of Cadillac Square, the Hammond Building, and city hall. The magnificent city hall was built in 1871 and was razed in 1961. There were four statues in the clock tower representing justice, industry, art, and commerce. Four statues of historic figures on the front of the building were salvaged and moved to Wayne State University where they are now in front of a parking structure.

Another early postcard shows the Pontchartrain, the city hall, and the Hammond Building on Cadillac Square. The 10-story Hammond Building was Detroit's first skyscraper. It was built in 1889 by George H. Hammond Sr. who used the ice-cooled refrigerated railroad car designed by Detroiter William Davis to transport meat from his packing plant to other cities. The Hammond Building was torn down in 1956.

Dime Bank and Pontchartrain Hotel, Detroit.

The Dime Bank Building is shown on this postcard with the Pontchartrain. The Pontchartrain is at the far left facing the Campus Martius and city hall. The Soldiers and Sailors Monument is in the center bottom of the postcard. The Dime Bank Building still exists, is now called the Griswold Place, and is being converted into condominiums.

PONTCHARTRAIN HOTEL AND HAMMOND BUILDING, BY NIGHT, DETROIT, MICH.

This is a dramatic, moonlight night view of the Pontchartrain with the Hammond Building across the street. When in action, the electric sign on top of one of the center buildings gave a description of the famous chariot race from the movie *Ben Hur*. The Soldiers and Sailors Monument is in the foreground.

Looking west in this rare postcard postmarked in 1919, one can see the Pontchartrain and the city hall. The Gayety Theater and several smaller hotels are also shown. The Pontchartrain had a short life, and it soon became obsolete partly because only some of the rooms had baths. It closed in January 1920, and was torn down a few months later. The First National Bank Building was constructed on the site.

The Brunswick Hotel was located at the corner of Grand River and Cass Avenues and was one of Detroit's many smaller hotels. It was owned by Harry L. Zeese and J. Milton Earle. Earle operated the hotel until 1915. There was an earlier Brunswick Hotel located at Griswold and State Streets that opened in 1878; by 1929 the David Stott Building was erected where the earlier hotel once stood.

The Berghoff Hotel opened in 1909, and this postcard of the Bohemian Room was postmarked in Chicago in 1911. The hotel was owned by W. D. C. Moebs and Company who also owned a large wholesale and retail cigar business and was opposite the Temple Theater and next to the Café Frontenac. The hotel was on the historic Monroe Block that was razed in 1990.

The Van Fleteren Hotel was located in Highland Park, not in Detroit as stated on the card. Highland Park is a suburb almost completely surrounded by Detroit, and it was there in 1910 that Henry Ford opened his Highland Park Ford Plant. The windows of the hotel saloon advertise Altes Lager. The hotel was owned by Emil Van Fleteren, a Belgian, who later was a builder in Grosse Pointe.

This is a night view of the Hotel Griswold, which was located at Grand River Avenue and Griswold Street. There was an earlier Hotel Griswold that was located at Congress and Griswold Streets but was torn down in 1895. The second hotel opened in 1910 and was where the Kiwanis Club, a community service organization, was founded January 21, 1915. It is now the site of a parking garage.

The Hotel Griswold billed their Pompeian Room as the only room of its kind in the city. It was predominantly red in color, and was one of four rooms that opened off the main café. This postcard was sent to a Mrs. J. R. Arnold of 1118 Columbia Avenue in Fort Wayne, Indiana.

The Hotel Griswold buffet was billed as the only one of its kind in the country. High-backed upholstered lounging benches (not shown) were provided for the use of guests. The refrigerated barrels of beer can be seen behind the bar as well as the vaults that stocked the fine wines and liquors. The room had a green color scheme.

The Hotel Charlevoix was only in business as a hotel for about 10 years. The structure was originally constructed for use as an office building and was owned by the Grinnell Realty Company. It opened as a hotel on Park Boulevard in 1912 but was altered and remodeled into an office building in 1922.

Hotel Statler, Detroit, Mich.

The Hotel Statler opened in January 1915 at Washington Boulevard and Bagley Street. It was designed by architect George B. Post, and the interior designer was Louis Rorimer. The hotel was built on the site of the John J. Bagley homestead that was owned then by a man named Arthur Fleming. This color penny postcard was postmarked May 22, 1916, showing how the hotel looked when it was new. The postcard says the Hotel Statler cost $3.5 million to build. There were 800 rooms with luxurious suites overlooking Grand Circus Park. At the time, there were only two other hotels in the chain founded by Ellsworth M. Statler. They were located in Buffalo and Cleveland. A new wing was added to the hotel in 1916, bringing the total number of rooms to 1,000—a first for Detroit. It was also the first hotel in the country to have central air conditioning and was the largest hotel in the Midwest.

HOTEL STATLER, HOTEL TULLER AND KRESGE BUILDING, GRAND CIRCUS PARK, DETROIT, MICH.

In this postcard, postmarked in 1918 and sent to Amsterdam, New York, the Hotel Statler, Hotel Tuller, and the Kresge Building can be seen from a view overlooking Woodward Avenue and Grand Circus Park. The Kresge Building was designed by Albert Kahn and is now called the Kales Building. Detroit entrepreneurs were trying to turn Washington Boulevard between Michigan Avenue and Grand Circus Park into a shopping area like New York's Fifth Avenue.

Washington Boulevard from Michigan Avenue, Detroit. Mich.

Statler Hotel.   David Whitney Bldg.

Here is the Book Building along with the Statler Hotel and the David Whitney Building as they appeared on Washington Boulevard looking from Michigan Avenue. The monument in the foreground was erected by the Daughters of the American Revolution to honor Gen. Alexander Macomb. This postcard was postmarked February 20, 1930, and was sent to a Mrs. Stow in Port Huron.

GRAND CIRCUS PARK, SHOWING WHITNEY BLDG., CADILLAC AND STATLER HOTELS, DETROIT, MICH.   105954

The Hotel Statler was a popular subject for postcards, and this one shows the hotel from Grand Circus Park with the Whitney Building on the left and the Book Cadillac in the distant center. This color postcard was postmarked July 26, 1928. It was sent to Viola Short at 246 Seymour Avenue in Derby, Connecticut.

597:–GRAND CIRCUS PARK SHOWING WASHINGTON BLVD. AND STATLER HOTEL. DETROIT. MICH.

Shown from Grand Circus Park is still another view of the Statler, situated between Washington Boulevard and Bagley Street. It advertised 1,000 attractive, air-conditioned guest rooms. The fabulous United Artists and the Michigan movie theaters, as well as the Hotel Tuller, can also be seen on this postcard.

240—Hotel Statler,
Detroit, Mich.

In another postcard of the Hotel Statler taken in the 1940s, one can see the Hotel Tuller behind it. They were both well known Detroit hotels and competitors during a time when Detroit was booming. During World War II, many employees were called to serve in the war effort, which caused staff shortages at all the hotels.

Hotel Statler

DETROIT

The Statler hotel chain had locations in six cities at the time this postcard of the Hotel Statler was designed. It features a Motor City car theme—men working on the assembly line—and also shows the Ambassador Bridge linking Detroit to Canada. It advertised that the hotel was near the J. L. Hudson Company and other department stores, and also near seven movie theaters and the famous Michigan Palace Supper Club.

This is an unused postcard of the Hotel Statler shown facing Grand Circus Park after it was sold to the Hilton chain. The card advertised free parking and family rates and stated the hotel was off the Bagley exit of the southbound John Lodge Expressway.

This postcard is from 1954 when the Hotel Statler was sold to the Hilton hotel chain and became the Statler Hilton. Since then, it has had a succession of owners and was renamed the Detroit Heritage Hotel in 1969. It finally closed in 1975. Red awnings were placed on the empty hotel windows for the Republican convention in 2000, and they remained there until 2002. The building was torn down in 2005 just in time for the Super Bowl in 2006.

The North Pole Hotel was located at Twelfth and Stanley Streets and the phone number was Walnut 2829 J. It was owned by Louis Chonoski, who immigrated to the United States from German Poland in 1878 and ran a saloon in Detroit in 1910. This postcard shows the hotel bar with a beautiful tin ceiling.

Another hotel from the same era as the North Pole Hotel was the Hermitage Hotel, which was located at Congress and Bates Streets "in the center of Detroit." The rooms were $1 and up, and the hotel was owned by Smith and Jones. This postcard is of the bar of the Hermitage Hotel about 1917.

Hotel Norton, Detroit, Mich.

The Hotel Norton, located at Griswold Street and Jefferson Avenue, opened in June 1918. Newspaper advertisements said it was near the business district and closest to the docks, interurban, and railroads. The hotel had 250 outside rooms with views of the Detroit River, the Canadian frontier, and the city of Detroit. There was a restaurant that accommodated 200 people. Charles W. Norton was the manager.

SKÅL!

SMÖRGÅSBORD
A Bit of Sweden — 410 GRISWOLD ST. — DETROIT, MICH.
Under the Direction of ERIC LUNDAHL

A Bit of Sweden was a restaurant in the Hotel Norton that served smorgasbord under the direction of Eric Lundahl. It advertised "half a block of good food" and was "recommended by Duncan Hines." Duncan Hines was a food critic who did restaurant ratings for travelers, and restaurants favorably listed in his book were given the Duncan Hines seal of approval.

Another of Detroit's small hotels was the 50-room Hotel Andoria, which was located at 6505 Third Street at West Grand Boulevard. It was located one block away from the Fisher and General Motors Buildings and offered rooms with or without baths. The hotel advertised that it had telephones in each room. In 1927, the resident manager was Sidney B. Pratt, and the tearoom was managed by Lillian Wagner.

Another large Detroit hotel was the Hotel Wolverine, which was built in 1920 and was located on Elizabeth and Witherell Streets, one block east of Woodward Avenue. It had twin towers and overlooked Grand Circus Park. Each of the 500 rooms had a tub and shower. A single room with bath was $3; a double was $5. The Tropics nightclub adjoined the restaurant.

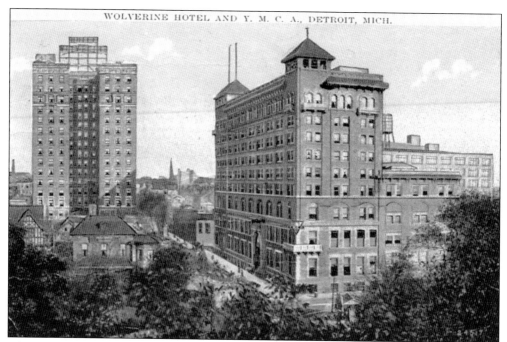

The Hotel Wolverine is shown here with the enormous YMCA building, built about 1908, in a postcard postmarked in 1929. The hotel was used as an emergency housing shelter in the late 1960s. Both the hotel and YMCA building were demolished in the 1990s, and the site is now the parking lot for Comerica Park where the Detroit Tigers play baseball.

Looking north from Grand Circus Park the Hotel Wolverine is seen on the far right in this 1950s postcard. The Fyfe Building and a DeSoto billboard are on one side of Woodward Avenue, and the Central Methodist Church is on the other. The Fyfe Building is a 14-story skyscraper built in 1919 in the neo-Gothic architectural style. Its primary use is now residential.

The Hotel Plaza was a 100-room hotel located at Madison Avenue and John R Street. All the rooms had baths. The proprietor was Frank E. Ellsworth who had managed the Western Newspaper Union from 1895 to 1912 prior to going into the hotel business. The telephone number was Cherry 4800. Ellsworth also owned the 239-room Henry Clay Hotel at 1538 Centre Street. The Henry Clay Hotel is now the Milner Hotel.

Another of Detroit's small hotels was the Hotel McGraw, which was located at 5605 Junction Street at the corner of McGraw Street in the ethnic Polish area of Detroit. This postcard was postmarked in 1935, and the back of the card reads, "You will always feel at home at the Hotel McGraw."

HOTEL BRIGGS
Adams Ave. at Grand Circus Park
Detroit, Michigan - Phone WO. 3-6800

The 18-story Hotel Briggs opened in the 1920s at Adams Avenue and Park Boulevard. It adjoined the Oriental Theater, the lobby of which was incorporated into the hotel. The Hotel Briggs was owned by Lester Briggs who was called a "boy millionaire" because of his many real estate investments. He died in his hotel in 1932 at the age of 40 after an illness that lasted two months.

The Hotel Roosevelt was built about 1923 and was located at 2250 Fourteenth Street across the street from the Michigan Central Depot, which was an ideal location for a hotel. The postcard says the 250-room hotel had "every accommodation for the traveler or tourist." The hotel had a restaurant, drug store, and barbershop. The empty building is still standing, and there is talk about turning it into condominiums.

One of Detroit's better known hotels was the Hotel Fort Shelby, which opened in June 1918 on West Lafayette. It was the first hotel in the world to offer servidor service to the guest rooms. These were cabinets built into the doors of the rooms that allowed room service or other deliveries to be made without disturbing the guests. John C. Thomson was the manager.

A 450-room addition, designed by Albert Kahn, was added to Hotel Fort Shelby in 1927. By the time this postcard was printed, the 900-room hotel was owned by the Albert Pick Hotels chain and called the Pick Fort Shelby. It closed in December 1973, reopened briefly in 1974, and is now slated for renovation.

"YOUR HOME AWAY FROM HOME"

LOBBY AND OFFICE

450 ROOMS

• LOUNGE ROOM •

HOTEL FAIRBAIRN, DETROIT, MICH.

The Hotel Fairbairn billed itself as "your home away from home." It was a hotel built for bachelors in 1923. It had a billiard room in the basement, a cafeteria, barber and tailor shops, and a laundry. The exterior was made of Indiana limestone and face brick in the Italian Renaissance style. P. R. Bierer was the hotel manager. A 1939 newspaper advertisement stated that the hotel offered "clean rooms for $5 a week with lots of hot water."

LOBBY, FIELD HOTEL, 445 FIELD AVE.—AT BELLE ISLE BRIDGE, DETROIT, MICHIGAN   116154

This postcard shows the lobby of the Field Hotel, which was located at 445 Field Avenue near the Belle Isle Bridge. Belle Isle was a popular spot for both residents and tourists and had a casino, boats and boat clubs, and picnicking areas. Rates at the hotel were $2 to $4 a day, and Ethel M. Kramer was the manager there in 1927.

GOTHAM HOTEL, JOHN R ST. AND ORCHESTRA PLACE
DETROIT, MICH.

The Gotham Hotel was located at John R Street and Orchestra Place. It was designed by Albert Kahn and built in 1924 by Albert Hartz. It had 200 rooms, all with a private bath, tub, or shower. In 1943, the owners were Irving Roane and John J. White, and the manager was W. H. "Bob" Robinson. The elegant Ebony dining room had fresh flowers daily. The hotel was a social center for the Detroit African American community in the area of Detroit then called Paradise Valley. Some of the famous guests were Sammy Davis Jr., Nat King Cole, Adam Clayton Powell, Joe Louis, B. B. King, the Harlem Globetrotters, Ella Fitzgerald, Erroll Garner, Duke Ellington, Count Basie, and Billie Holiday. Actress Marla Gibbs once worked at the Gotham Hotel as a switchboard operator. The hotel closed in 1962 and John J. White died soon after while awaiting trial on federal gambling charges. Some said he died of a broken heart. The hotel was torn down in 1964. Paradise Valley is gone now and only Orchestra Hall remains.

Book-Cadillac Hotel, Detroit, Mich.   10

When the Book Cadillac Hotel opened on December 8, 1924, it was the tallest building in Michigan and the largest hotel in the world. It was built by the Book brothers—J. B., Herbert, and Frank—and was designed by Detroit architect Louis Kamper. The hotel was built on the site of four earlier hotels, the first being a 20-room inn built by Nathaniel Champe, a veteran of the War of 1812. The four figures on the facade of the hotel are Chief Pontiac; Robert Navarre; Antoine Laumet, sieur de Lamothe Cadillac; and Gen. Anthony Wayne. The grand staircase was made of Breche Violette marble and the beams were made of solid walnut. There were Venetian bronze chandeliers, chairs covered in Italian velvet, and Sevres vases. The two-story grand ballroom had half-ton crystal chandeliers, gold leaf ceilings, and an electric fountain, complete with matching rose-colored drapes and carpets. This grand hotel has been the subject of entire books, was the place to be seen in Detroit, and was where many celebrities stayed. It had 13 passenger elevators, a post office, an express and railroad ticket office, a telegraph office, and radio stations.

This postcard postmarked 1932 is the main lobby of the Book Cadillac. It was sent by George T. Hayman who was attending a convention of Osteopathic Physicians and Surgeons that were meeting in Parlor F of the hotel. The hotel had 1,200 rooms, which made it ideal for conventions. All of the guest rooms were located on the upper-23 stories of the hotel, and they all had private baths.

Another undated postcard shows the elegant Venetian Dining Room of the Book Cadillac with its beautiful crystal chandeliers. The hotel had four restaurants, including a less opulent Café Cadillac. The Venetian Dining Room later became the Book Casino, which was famous for entertainment and fine music.

This undated postcard features the Book Cadillac's beautiful Blue Room. Special luncheons were offered there as well as deluxe dinners. It was a gay setting for dinners or after-theater parties. Dinner and dancing was offered nightly from 7:00 p.m. to 1:00 a.m., except on Sunday, with music by Jean Goldkette's Book Cadillac Dance Orchestra. Goldkette is not well known today, but he was famous in the 1920s and was called "the prince of jazz."

127 WASHINGTON BOULEVARD, INDUSTRIAL BANK BUILDING AND BOOK CADILLAC HOTEL, DETROIT, MICH.

In this view from Washington Boulevard, the Industrial Bank Building is seen along with the Book Cadillac Hotel. The postcard was postmarked in 1928. Back in those days the hotels kept an accurate history on each guest, and if one should happen to be staying there on one's birthday a birthday cake would thoughtfully be placed in the guest's room.

Fay M. Thomas was the general manager of the Book Cadillac when this postcard was printed. He came to Detroit from New Orleans in 1942 where he had managed the Hotel Roosevelt. He stayed on as the general manager when the Sheraton chain took over in 1951. It was the second-largest hotel in the Sheraton chain, and $1 million was spent by Sheraton to refurbish it.

The Book Cadillac is shown on a map with Detroit as a prominent red dot in another postcard from the same era when Thomas was general manager. The hotel was still the headquarters for major conventions and other events in Detroit. The elegant presidential suite was used by many presidents and other dignitaries.

The Motor City is again the theme of this 1950s postcard when the Book Cadillac was part of the Sheraton chain and was called the Sheraton Cadillac Hotel. Some of the renovations done to modernize the hotel in the 1950s included replacing the grand marble staircase entrance with dual escalators. The only public rooms left untouched by the remodeling efforts of the 1950s were the Grand Ballroom and the Italian Garden. By that time the name of the Café Cadillac was changed to the Café Caprice reflecting an effort to make the hotel more contemporary.

THE SHERATON-CADILLAC HOTEL
Detroit 31,   Michigan

This postcard was postmarked in 1955. Some of the highlights of the Sheraton Cadillac Hotel listed on the back of the card were a men's grill and a men's bar, reflecting the fact that many of its guests were businessmen. The hotel had beauty parlors, tearooms, and shops in the arcade for women.

52

The Motor City automobile theme is again featured on this postcard of the Sheraton Cadillac Hotel. This 3¢ postcard was postmarked in 1957. Detroit was then the automobile capitol of the world, having celebrated the 50th anniversary of the American automobile 11 years earlier in 1946 with an Automotive Golden Jubilee which lasted 12 days.

Old fashioned streetlights line Washington Boulevard across the street from the Sheraton Cadillac Hotel in the 1950s. This is the view from Michigan Avenue. The main entrance of the hotel faced Washington Boulevard. The phone number then was Woodward 1-8000. Buses left for the Willow Run Airport every 20 minutes.

From another angle looking towards Michigan Avenue, the Sheraton Cadillac Hotel is seen from Washington Boulevard in the 1950s. Part of the Hotel Wolverine can be seen on the far right. Detroit celebrated its 250th anniversary in 1951, and the banners on Washington Boulevard were part of the festivities. The 250th anniversary logo featured a French fleur-de-lis, a British lion, and an American eagle, symbolizing the three governments that ruled the city.

The old fashioned streetlights are lit up across the street from the Sheraton Cadillac in a 1950s postcard that offers a unique night view. The hotel became the Radisson Cadillac in 1978, and then closed. All the contents were liquidated in 1986, and the once-grand and lively hotel sat vacant for 20 years.

HOTEL WEBSTER HALL
CASS AT PUTNAM
DETROIT, MICH.

Another large hotel, Webster Hall, was built at the same time as the Book Cadillac Hotel, but it was overshadowed by the larger, more opulent Book Cadillac Hotel. Webster Hall was located at Cass Avenue, Putnam Street, and Woodward Avenue in the city's art center. It had 800 rooms, two coffee shops, a ballroom, meeting rooms, and a large swimming pool in the basement. It was a residential hotel for men and women located close to the Detroit Public Library, the Detroit Institute of Arts, and Wayne State University. It operated in bankruptcy in the 1930s and its 220 employees staged a sit–down strike in March 1937, leaving the 650 hotel guests to cope as best they could. Only the drug store and cigar shop continued to operate during the strike. In the mid-1940s Wayne State University took over the hotel, renamed it Mackenzie Hall, and used it as a dormitory, recreation, and office building. It was imploded in the mid-1990s and is now the site of a parking garage.

Webster Hall is behind the Detroit Public Library on the right in this 1940s postcard. It is dwarfed by the library and the Maccabees Building. The Maccabees Building was the home of WXYZ radio and later, in 1948, WXYZ television. Prominent radio personalities in Detroit at the time were Dick Osgood, Frances Langford, Paul Whiteman, Fred Wolf, Ed McKenzie, Mickey Shorr, and "the Lady of Charm" Edyth Fern Melrose.

There was not much that was majestic about the Majestic Hotel. The architect was J. Phillip McDonnell. The 250-room hotel was built in 1925 and was located at 160 West Montcalm Street at Clifford Street. A barbershop, the Pow Wow saloon, and a restaurant named the Clif-Mont Café were on the street level. Richard Callahan was the manager there in 1930.

Shown here in a postcard postmarked in 1942 is the Wardell Apartment Hotel that was built in 1926. It was designed by Harley and Ellington who designed the Stroh Brewery and the Horace Rackham Building. It was named for Fred Wardell, founder of Detroit's Eureka Vacuum Cleaner Company. Residential hotels were places people could stay for extended periods of times, usually a month or more. Diego Rivera lived there for about a year while he worked on his famous mural at the Detroit Institute of Arts.

The Wardell Apartment Hotel later became the Park Shelton Hotel as shown in this undated color postcard. The Park Shelton Hotel offered luxurious transient accommodations and some apartments, television, and radio on all floors as well as ice machines and free parking. Some famous residents of the hotel were Bob Hope, George Burns, Gracie Allen, and Raymond Burr who stayed there while appearing in Detroit. The Park Shelton Hotel is currently being renovated and sold as condominiums.

THE SEWARD — Seward at Woodward Ave. — DETROIT, MICH.

Another of the downtown Detroit hotels was the Seward, which was located at 59 Seward Street at Woodward Avenue and opened around 1926. The manager in 1930 was William E. Snyder. It was billed as "Detroit's Leading Uptown Hotel."

The Prenford Hotel opened about 1925 and was located at 11626 Woodward Avenue at Woodland Street in the North Woodward district. The postcard says it was in Detroit, but it was actually in Highland Park. It had 150 rooms, catered to bachelors, and advertised itself as being "refined and dignified." P. M. Butler was the manager there in the 1950s.

This is a black-and-white postcard of the Detroiter Hotel, which was built as the Hotel Savoy in 1926 and then renamed the Hotel LaSalle. It was renamed the Detroiter Hotel in 1931. It was 12 stories high and had 800 rooms, 18 corner suites, and a two-story penthouse apartment. It was designed by Paul Kamper, son of architect Louis Kamper, and was located at Woodward Avenue and Adelaide Street.

The Detroiter Hotel is shown again in a 1940s postcard when it was a commercial hotel that had 750 rooms with baths. In the 1950s, it became Carmel Hall, a residence for the elderly, which was run by the Carmelite Sisters of the Sick and Infirm of Germantown, New York. The building was imploded March 2, 1996, and new townhouses have since been constructed on the site.

Another hotel on Cadillac Square was the Barlum Tower and Hotel. It opened in February 1927. It was a 20-story structure with 612 guest rooms, and each had a private bath. The exterior was pure white terra-cotta. Ornate Venetian décor dominated the hotel lobby. It catered to theatrical guests who were appearing on stage in Detroit. These included actors, musicians, ice skaters, and striptease artists.

Another postcard shows the Barlum Tower and Hotel as it was situated on Cadillac Square. The land was originally owned by Lydia Hullibert who sold it in 1817 for $100. The hotel was built by John H. Barlum who also owned the Barlum Steamship Company and was the president of the Detroit Street Railways (DSR). He lost the hotel during the Depression in the 1930s.

This is the Barlum Tower and Hotel after its name changed to the Henrose Hotel in 1958. It advertised free parking for transient guests. It was owned by Henry Keywell and his wife, Rose, hence the name Henrose. They put $600,000 into improvements. It was eventually bought in 1964 by a Washington syndicate and renamed the Embassy, and is now the New Cadillac Square Apartments.

HENROSE HOTEL

HOTEL YORBA — 4020 West Lafayette — 2 Blocks West of West Grand Boulevard — DETROIT, MICHIGAN

The Hotel Yorba opened in 1926. It was and still is a transient and residential hotel located on West Lafayette Boulevard two blocks west of West Grand Boulevard near the Ambassador Bridge. It had 300 rooms and a coffee shop. "The Yorba" was the title of a song by the White Stripes, a British music group, in 2001. The song was supposedly written in one of the rooms of the hotel.

FORT WAYNE HOTEL
DETROIT, MICHIGAN
Temple and Cass Aves.

This 1950s-era postcard is of the Fort Wayne Hotel, which was located at Temple Street, then called Bagg Street, and Cass Avenue in Detroit and opened in May 1926. It had 300 rooms and 300 baths and was home to the Café Burgundy. When it opened a single room with a bath was $2. It is now the American Fort Wayne Hotel, one of the older Detroit hotels still operating but under a slightly different name.

MASONIC TEMPLE SHRINE CLUB   FORT WAYNE HOTEL, DETROIT. MICHIGAN

The Fort Wayne Hotel is shown here next to the Masonic Temple Shrine Club. The Detroit Masonic Temple was designed by George Mason and was also opened in 1926. It cost $7 million to build, and is the largest Masonic temple in the world. It has three ballrooms, a cathedral, and the theater seats over 4,000 people.

The Detroit-Leland Hotel opened in April 1927 on Bagley Street at Cass Avenue. It had 22 stories and 800 rooms with air conditioning, a dining room, and a coffee shop. The coffee shop was in the basement. The street level had 11 stores connected by an arcade. It was designed by C. W. Rapp and George L. Rapp in Italian Renaissance style. Its exterior is granite, terra-cotta, and face brick.

This postcard is of the Grenadier dining room and lounge at the Detroit-Leland Hotel. The hotel was named for Henry M. Leland who was the founder of the Cadillac Automobile Company in Detroit in 1901. He later sold his company to Will Durant's General Motors Corporation, and worked for Durant as head of the Cadillac division.

COFFEE SHOP

GRENADIER DINING ROOM and LOUNGE BAR

DETROIT LELAND

Detroit-Leland Hotel
DETROIT, MICH.

THE LOBBY

COLONIAL BALL ROOM

Some of the rooms of the Detroit-Leland Hotel are shown on this postcard postmarked in 1943 with the hotel in the center. One can see the coffee shop, the lobby, the Grenadier dining room and lounge bar, and the colonial ballroom. Negotiations between the automobile companies and the United Auto Workers were held here. The Ford Motor Company and the United Auto Workers met at the 50-foot bargaining table in the English Room in 1958.

Still another postcard from about 1960 shows the Detroit-Leland Hotel with the Detroit Edison, now DTE Energy, headquarters building in the distance behind the hotel. The hotel has since been renovated and is still open as the Leland Hotel.

The Whittier Hotel was built in 1926 during Detroit's building boom. The 13-story, renaissance-style building was another apartment hotel that included services such as restaurants, dry cleaners, and maid service for the residents. It was designed by Charles N. Agree and is located on Burns Drive near Jefferson Avenue across from Belle Isle. Because the site was so close to the Detroit River, the architect consulted Japanese engineers who were skilled in building on soggy ground on how to build the hotel. This was once one of Detroit's finer hotels. Among the famous guests who stayed here were Mae West, Cornelia Otis Skinner, writer Damon Runyon, the Beatles, the Rolling Stones, and playboy Horace Dodge Jr. and his movie star wife Gregg Sherwood. It was the headquarters for the Gold Cup and Silver Cup powerboat races. In 1969, it became a senior residence owned by the Michigan Baptist Homes and Development Company and was called Whittier Towers. It was put on the National Register of Historic Places in 1985. The building closed in 2001 and is currently empty awaiting development into condominiums.

The Belcrest Hotel, built in 1926 at 5440 Cass Avenue, was and still is a residential hotel that overlooks the Art Center on Woodward Avenue and is a short distance from Wayne State University. It was designed by Charles N. Agree who also designed the Whittier Hotel. It is on the Michigan State Register of Historic Sites and the National Register of Historic Places. This postcard is an interior view, probably of the lobby of the hotel in the 1930s.

THE BELCREST, 5440 CASS AVENUE, DETROIT, MICHIGAN

The Hotel Garfield was located at John R and Garfield Streets. It was managed by James Kordoulis in 1931, and later it was owned by Randolph W. Wallace. Randolph and his wife, Ora, were prominent black business owners and also owned a grocery store. These businesses were part of Detroit's Paradise Valley.

The smart, intimate Wal-Ha Room was located in the Hotel Garfield and featured entertainment nightly. This color postcard dates from the 1950s when it was a popular part of the lively night life of Paradise Valley. It was still in business and called the Garfield Lounge in the early 1970s.

The Randora Motor Hotel was located at 98 Garfield Street, near Woodward Avenue, and advertised that it had "the conveniences of a motel combined with the services of a hotel." A 1953 Cadillac Eldorado is parked in front of the hotel. All rooms had air conditioning, free television and radios, and tiled baths. Typical rooms are shown on the postcard. Studio beds in hotels became popular around 1940 because the hotel room could be used as a living room or parlor during the day.

Howard Johnson's Downtown Motor Lodge was at Washington Boulevard and Michigan Avenue. It had 300 rooms, an enclosed rooftop pool, and a sauna. It also had five floors of indoor parking for its guests. There was another Howard Johnson's Motor Lodge on West Grand Boulevard just west of Second Avenue that was used as a residence for student nurses by Henry Ford Hospital in the 1970s after the hotel closed. That building was demolished in 1997.

This color postcard from about 1960 is of the Steak Room, one of two dining rooms of the Holiday Inn Downtown, which was located at 1331 Trumbull Street between Porter and Abbott Streets. It was four blocks away from the old Tiger stadium, Cobo Hall, and the downtown shopping area.

The Hotel St. Regis is located at West Grand Boulevard and Cass Avenue and is in the New Center area of Detroit. It was once across the street from the General Motors Building before the General Motors Corporation purchased the Renaissance Center. The hotel featured handcrafted European antiques and elegant dining. It opened in the 1960s and the phone number then was Trinity 3-3000; it now has a 1-800 number.

Town Motel
2127 WEST GRAND BLVD., DETROIT 8, MICH.

The Town Motel is shown in this 1950s postcard. It had 26 deluxe units, kitchens, radios, and televisions. It is located at 2127 West Grand Boulevard one block east of Grand River Avenue and is still in business. At the time this postcard was printed, the phone number was Tyler 8-6353 and it was located in Detroit 8, Michigan.

126 Luxurious Air-Conditioned Rooms—Heated Pool

HARLAN HOUSE MOTEL

AT LODGE EXPRESSWAY AND WEST GRAND BLVD. – DETROIT

The Harlan House Motel was located at the Lodge Expressway and West Grand Boulevard in the 1960s. It was across the street from Henry Ford Hospital and less than two blocks away from what was then the General Motors Building. It had 126 rooms, a heated pool, free television and radio, a restaurant, and a cocktail lounge.

The Bali-Hi Motel is another 1960s-era motel located at 10501 East Jefferson Avenue across the street from the Detroit Waterworks Park. The phone number then was Valley 2-3500. The motel advertised free coffee and newspapers, foam rubber mattresses, free television and telephones, tiled baths, and it also had kitchenettes available. The motel is still open.

Two

DETROIT'S RESTAURANTS

Detroit is a city known for its restaurants, especially for its many ethnic restaurants. Among the ethnic restaurants included are German, Italian, Chinese, Swedish, and Greek, though there are many others such as those specializing in Polish, Hungarian, Middle Eastern, and Indian cuisine. While it would have been ideal to include postcards of all the early Detroit restaurants, this was not possible in terms of the numbers of the early restaurants and the availability of postcards. In 1888, there were about 90 restaurants listed in the Detroit city directory. Many were small, family run restaurants. The earliest Detroit restaurant still in business is the Roma Café, which is located in the historic Eastern Market. It opened in 1890 in a building that dates to 1888 where the Marazza family ran a boardinghouse. Mrs. Marazza was a fine cook, and she expanded her business into a restaurant that she named the Roma Café. It is still being run under that name over 100 years later. Another early restaurant that is still in business is the Dakota Inn Rathskeller. It opened as a tiny, three-stool Rathskeller on August 1, 1933. This German restaurant expanded and today seats 145 patrons. It has been run by the same family since it opened. The restaurants included in this chapter run the gamut from self-serve to smorgasbord. Also shown are some of the elegant dining venues such as the Roostertail, the Top of the Flame, and the London Chop House.

The Roma Café is Detroit's oldest restaurant. The building itself dates back to 1888. The restaurant is located seven minutes away from downtown Detroit in the historic Eastern Market at Riopelle and Erskine Streets, and it features Italian and American cuisine. There are three dining rooms, and an Italian buffet is served on Monday nights. It was founded in 1890 as a boardinghouse by the Marazza family, and Mrs. Marazza, who was a fine cook, later opened her own restaurant and called it the Roma Café. It was bought by John Battaglia and Morris Sossi in 1918, and Sossi bought the restaurant from Battaglia's widow within one year and became sole owner. It has been run by the Sossi family ever since, and Janet Sossi Belcoure is the current manager.

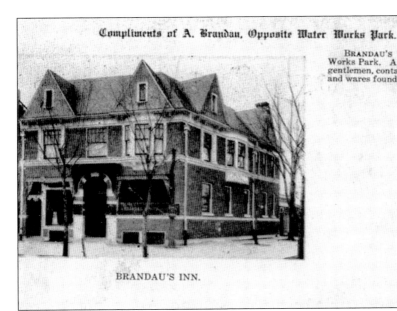

BRANDAU'S INN, Opposite Water Works Park. A Cafe for ladies and gentlemen, containing all conveniences and wares found in a first class resort.

BRANDAU'S INN.

Brandau's Inn is shown on this 1890 private 1¢ postcard. It was called private because no writing other than the address was permitted on the front of the card. The inn was a café for ladies and gentlemen located across the street from Waterworks Park. It was owned by Andrew Brandau. His son, Louis, later operated a confectionery at the same location, which he ran for 50 years.

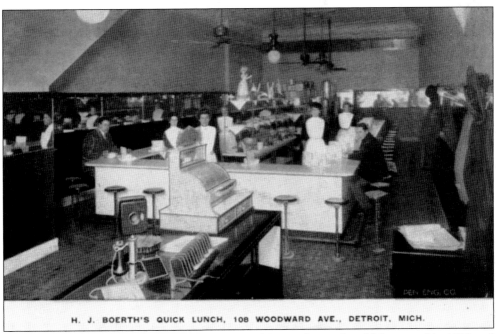

H. J. BOERTH'S QUICK LUNCH, 108 WOODWARD AVE., DETROIT, MICH.

This is another private 1¢ postcard of H. J. Boerth's Quick Lunch, which opened in 1901 and was located at 108 Woodward Avenue. It was owned by Henry J. Boerth who also was the owner of the H. J. Pie Baking Company on Sixteenth Street. He probably served his pies in his restaurant. Note the early telephone on the counter next to the cash register.

73

H. L. Bowles's Baltimore Lunch was located at 81 Woodward Avenue. This *c.* 1910 restaurant was one of a chain of restaurants across the country that marked the beginning of the fast food business. Other restaurants in the chain were located in Springfield, Massachusetts; Hartford, Connecticut; Syracuse, New York; Buffalo, New York; Milwaukee, Wisconsin; Providence, Rhode Island; Toledo, Ohio; Duluth, Minnesota; and Pawtucket, Rhode Island.

Kartsen's was both a self-service cafeteria and a full service restaurant that opened on February 16, 1915, at 1548 South Woodward Avenue, just south of Grand Circus Park. It advertised that it was air conditioned and had "pleasant prices." They claimed to be the oldest cafeteria in Michigan. The Cascade Room offered waitress and bar service from 11:00 a.m. until 8:00 p.m.

The Avenue Servself was located at 84 Woodward Avenue at the corner of Larned. The dishes were displayed on large serving counters from which customers selected their food. The clientele was primarily visitors and tourists off the streetcars and the steamboats that were docked nearby. It was owned by Messrs. Brennan, Fitzgerald, and Sinks.

The Majestic Servself was located in the basement of the Majestic Building. It was ideally located and the largest of its kind. This "quick lunch" restaurant made the claim that they could serve 1,000 people per hour. This servself was also owned by Messrs. Brennan, Fitzgerald, and Sinks.

The Majestic Building is the large building on the left in this *c.* 1910 postcard. It was constructed in 1896 and was Detroit's second skyscraper. This is where the Majestic Servself was located. After a quick lunch at the Majestic Servself, tourists could go on the roof of the Majestic Building to get a good view of the city. The building was demolished in 1962.

Otto A. Huck owned the Log Cabin restaurant, located at 65 Michigan Avenue, from 1907 to 1912. It was across the street from the Cadillac Hotel. Huck came to Detroit in 1892 from Alsace-Lorraine and also owned the Schiller Restaurant from 1905 to 1907 in partnership with his brothers. He later bought the Westwood Symphony Gardens, a large outdoor ballroom, and the Westwood Otto Inn in Dearborn.

EMIL HUCK'S INN — GRAND RIVER AT 7 MILE ROAD — DETROIT, MICH.

Otto A. Huck had three brothers: August, Victor, and Emil. Emil and his sons owned the Huck's Redford Inn located at Grand River Avenue and Seven Mile Road. The restaurant had been the old Club Ackmur, which had been closed because of gambling activities, and it opened as a restaurant in 1939. The restaurant is shown on this color postcard in the 1940s. The building was set on nicely landscaped grounds and was famous for its fish, frog legs, chicken, and steak dinners. They grew their own vegetables on their farm and advertised air conditioned dining and banquet rooms. This busy restaurant had two phone numbers: Redford 9549 and Redford 1370. Emil also opened a second restaurant called Huck's Lakeshore Restaurant on Jefferson Avenue in St. Clair Shores, which opened shortly before his death in 1961.

This postcard is of the bar of Marquette's Café that was located at Six Mile Road and Woodward Avenue. It was owned by John Marquette about 1915. The bar shown on the postcard was reputed to be one of the longest in the country. They specialized in frog and chicken dinners and billed themselves as "Detroit's most popular dining place." Marquette's Café was formerly the Ardussi Café that was operated by Constant G. Ardussi who specialized in French and Italian cooking. Old Detroit families gathered there for Sunday dinners, and it was closely linked with the development of the automobile industry. It is said that the General Motors Corporation was organized at a dinner table in the Ardussi Café and that many early car races used the café as their starting point. The building was remodeled for use as a bank and then torn down in 1922 so that the street could be widened by 52 feet.

Another postcard from about 1890 shows the interior of the Cream of Michigan Café located at 20 Monroe Avenue. This was a saloon located on the famous Monroe Block, which was off Woodward Avenue. There were several owners listed for this address; two of them were G. H. Gies in 1888 and Burns and Palmer in 1904. Prior to World War I, most saloons served food at lunchtime.

Smith's Restaurant or Al Smith's Lunch, owned by Albert R. Smith, billed itself as the finest lunch room in Detroit. It was another cafeteria-style restaurant. Originally on Bates Street, this postcard shows the restaurant when it was located at Cadillac Square around 1910, a location that was strategically placed between the city and county buildings practically guaranteeing customers would appear at lunchtime.

Glaser's Edelweiss Café was at Broadway and John R Streets. This is a view, postmarked in 1917, with the restaurant on the left of Pingree Square. Detroit had a large German population with many restaurants catering to German food tastes. The restaurant was owned by Charlie Glaser who established a stammtisch, which was a long oak table where the writers and artists of Detroit would gather to discuss current events.

MAIN DINING ROOM   GLASER'S EDELWEISS CAFE   BROADWAY AT JOHN R. STREET DETROIT, MICH.

This postcard is of the main dining room of Glaser's Edelweiss Café, but the writer of this postcard, which is postmarked March 3, 1914, stated the restaurant took up the entire building. World War I brought changes to the restaurant's menu and German fried potatoes became American fried potatoes. The restaurant later moved to larger quarters at Monroe Avenue and Library Street.

Fischer's Alt Heidelberg Restaurant was located at 1250 Washington Boulevard. It is listed in the 1912 Detroit city directory. This was another restaurant specializing in delicious German cooking and it served wine, beer, and liquor. There was music and dancing in the second floor dining room. The jovial fellow with the beer glass is toasting *zur gesundheit* or "to your health."

The Café Frontenac opened in December 1913. It was located at 16–26 Monroe Avenue next to the Berghoff Hotel and had an Italian Garden Room (pictured) and a Tuxedo Grill Room. The restaurant offered musical entertainment every night.

81

Joe Muer's Oyster House was a legendary Detroit restaurant founded in 1929 on Gratiot Avenue in Detroit's east side German colony. It was founded on the site of Anthony Muer's cigar factory. The restaurant was known for its seafood, steaks, and chops. It closed in 1998 partly because three martini lunches and thick steaks were out of fashion and no longer a tax deductible business expense. The building was torn down in 2002. There was a Michigan historical marker placed on the site in 1981 that was later stolen.

The patriarch of the Muer family was Anthony (Tony) Muer who manufactured 5¢ cigars that he called Tony's Ponies. Shown on this postcard is the Muer family—Joe Jr., Joe Sr., Bill, and Tom. Joe Sr. died in 1958 and his son Bill took over the restaurant. Bill was a bachelor. Bill's nephew Joe was running the restaurant when it closed in 1998.

Dakota Inn Rathskeller
17324 John R
Detroit, Michigan

The Dakota Inn Rathskeller opened August 1, 1933, and it is still run by the same family. It was founded by Karl Kurz who modeled the restaurant into a German-style rathskeller like the one in his native Wiekersheim, Germany. The servers wear traditional German-style clothing, and the restaurant is filled with German beer steins. The restaurant was listed on the Michigan State Register of Historic Sites on June 30, 1988.

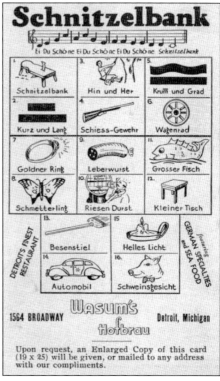

Still another German restaurant was Wasum's Hofbrau, which was located at 1564 Broadway Street between the Capitol Theater Building and Grand Circus Park. It specialized in German and seafood and had German beer on tap. It opened in December 1936. The owner was Hans H. Wasum who was the former manager of the Harmonie Club.

There were three Brass Rails in Detroit—at Adams and Grand Circus Park, at Michigan Avenue and Griswold Street, and at Woodward Avenue and the Boulevard. *Life* magazine described the Brass Rails as "Detroit's restaurants to fit your purse." They were open 365 days a year and served everything from sandwiches to steak dinners. Along with dinner came big shows with a chorus line, vocalists, and comedians.

Frame's Tea Room was located at 1439 Farmer Street in the heart of downtown. It was built to resemble a Colonial cottage and served luncheons, tea, and dinner. This advertising postcard from the 1930s was sent to V. J. Unsoldi of 1300 Broadway Street in Detroit and was signed by Katherine Ellen Frame who was the restaurant's owner.

The Old Cow Shed was popular in the 1930s and was known for steaks and chicken. It also offered dancing and entertainment. It was located at 30 Clifford Street and was owned and operated by Joe Monteith and George Planck. The manager was C. W. Holden.

Hall's Café, owned by Jimmy Hall, was located at 135 Lafayette Boulevard, a half block from city hall, and it specialized in seafood, steaks, chops, and fine liquors. The grill and bar and Miami Room are shown here in this 1930s color postcard.

Smorgasbord, or a buffet table laden with fish, meat, cheese, and other delicacies, was served at the Stockholm Restaurant at Jefferson Avenue and Rivard. The restaurant opened in 1939 in a 125-year-old house. It was owned by Siggan Sjunneson who was born in Stockholm, Sweden. Sjunneson, a widow, maintained a penthouse apartment in the restaurant and enjoyed travel and fine dining. Her late husband, John, was a General Motors Corporation executive.

The Stockholm Restaurant advertised that it was recommended by Duncan Hines and was considered one of Detroit's finest restaurants. It had five dining rooms. Names of many celebrities could be found in the guest book. It was sold in 1962 to the Chicago owners of a Playboy key club.

This 1940s-era color postcard pictures a theme restaurant, the Chick Inn, which was located at 9910 Telegraph Road between West Chicago and Plymouth Roads. The phone was Kenwood 1-9501. The restaurant specialized in southern fried chicken but also served steaks, chops, frog legs, and barbecued ribs.

The Paradiso Café was open from about 1929 until the 1960s. The original owners were cousins Frank Raiti and Gaspare Simonte. Simonte's wife, Anna, ran the kitchen. Anna later divorced Simonte and married Raiti. The restaurant was located at 17630 Woodward Avenue just north of McNichols Road, and the menu featured Italian food. The building was destroyed by fire in the 1990s.

Another 1940s-era dining and dancing establishment was the Palm Beach Café, which was located at 15414 Wyoming Avenue at James Couzens Highway. The highway was named for James Couzens who was the 50th mayor of the city of Detroit. In addition to dining, there were two floor shows nightly and three on Sunday.

The Sea Food Grotto was in business for about 30 years, first at 212 West Grand River Avenue and later at West Seven Mile Road at Telegraph Road. They billed themselves as "Detroit's exclusive sea food restaurant," but they also served steaks, chops, fowl, and game. In 1939, the owner was James C. Constand.

The original Scotty's Fish and Chips was located at 14945 Livernois Avenue at Chalfonte Street. Scotty was Alfred K. Wood, a Scotsman and former Windsor, Ontario, police officer, who also ran a meat market along with serving up fish and chips. There was another Scotty's restaurant at Outer Drive and Plymouth Road. Wood was also the manager of several motels, including the Aero Inn in Detroit.

Greektown is a popular area of Detroit, home to Greek restaurants and a casino. The Grecian Gardens was a popular Greektown restaurant located at 562 Monroe Avenue in the heart of Greektown. The main dining room is shown here in a 1950s-era postcard. There was also a private banquet room called the Athenian. It was owned by Gust Colocasides who was investigated for gambling, which was illegal then and is now a flourishing industry.

THE NAU'S SNO-WHITE

The Nau's Sno-White Dining Room was another 1950s-era restaurant, located at 18944 Grand River Avenue (U.S. Route 16) in northwest Detroit. The phone number was Broadway 3-4488. They advertised fine food, music, carry-out service, ice carvings, and specialized in catering and parties.

Carson's was a steak and prime roast rib house and cocktail lounge located at 6001 Woodward Avenue. The phone number was Trinity 4-0417. There were three private dining rooms. This is how the restaurant looked about 1950. It was owned by James Carson, who was active in the Greek community and who previously had owned the New Olympia restaurant. Carson died in 1975 and is buried in Greece.

Another 1950s-era restaurant was Krager's, located at 13158 Gratiot Avenue, which served German specialties and had a private room available for parties. Printed on the postage area of this spectra color postcard is "we will gladly affix stamp. Address and hand to server." The owner was Frank A. Krager who in 1939 owned a beer garden at 7411 Gratiot.

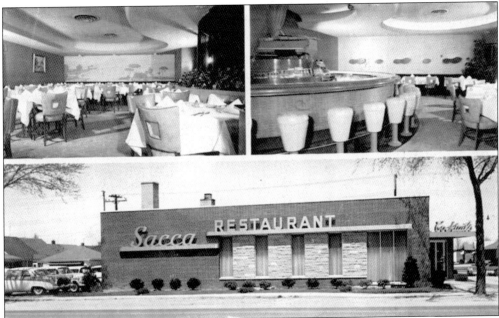

Sacca restaurant and supper club was at 18800 West McNichols Road in northwest Detroit and opened in 1955. The plush restaurant offered 55 entries and prepared special dishes tableside. According to a newspaper review, one could get a splendid meal at Sacca's for $4 or $5 in 1959. In August 1959, the restaurant burned down and one of the four owners was charged with arson.

Jerry Schoenith's Roostertail, located at 100 Marquette Drive, was one of Detroit's great restaurants. When it was built in 1958, it was ultra-modern, and the bar had a view of the Detroit River. Entertainers such as Tony Bennett, Peggy Lee, and the Supremes performed there and gourmet dinners were served Las Vegas style. The upper deck was reserved for Motown acts and the lower deck was used for the over-30 crowd.

This is the beautiful entry to the Roostertail's multi-level dining and cocktail areas as it looked when it opened. The Roostertail was an entertainment complex with motorized tram service throughout their pink-lighted parking area. Today it is strictly a catering and private party venue, hosting many of the city's top events.

The Anchor Inn restaurants were a chain located in Riverview, Clawson, and Bay City, as well as in Bradenton Beach, Florida, about 1960. There also was a restaurant in the Korvette Shopping Center on Telegraph and West Chicago Roads in Detroit. This color postcard shows some of their menu offerings that included fried shrimp, chicken, pickerel fillet, and ham steak. Roast chicken, biscuits, and gravy were served on Sundays only.

Another of Detroit's Italian restaurants, pictured here about 1960, was Perini's, which was located at 10721 Whittier Street. It was owned by Paul J. Perini. This was a moderately-priced spaghetti house that offered carry-out service but also had a room for private parties.

Eastman's Gaslight Room was located at Grand River Avenue and Bagley Street. The phone was Woodward 2-1020. It was owned by William and Beverly Eastman. This postcard shows a *c.* 1962 red and white Chevrolet parked in front of the restaurant as well as two views of the News Room dining room.

Overlooking the Detroit River . . . the Bangkok Cocktail Lounge, garden and unique Tempura Ba.

One of many beautiful views from the "Top" . . . Belle Isle and east toward the St. Clair River.

One of the places to go for special occasions was the Top of the Flame that was on the 26th floor of the Michigan Consolidated Gas Building at 1 Woodward Avenue. It opened in April 1963, and offered customers panoramic views of the Detroit River and Canada while they dined. It was operated by Stouffer's and specialized in Eastern (Thai) cookery as well as American cuisine. It closed in 1977.

The London Chop House was one of Detroit's most venerable and expensive restaurants. It was located on West Congress Street across the street from the Caucus Club where Barbra Streisand got her start in 1961. Les Gruber owned both restaurants at that time. Caricatures of the famous people who ate at the London Chop House lined the walls. Some of the drawings were of John Barrymore, Errol Flynn, Tallulah Bankhead, and Gary Cooper. All the drawings were created by Hy Vogel, a local artist. The caricatures were auctioned off in 1992. Frank Sinatra and Henry Ford II also dined there. Zero Mostel is said to have jumped on a table in the restaurant and said, "Mr. Gruber, your chopped herring is a poem." The restaurant was famous for its steaks and for the huge wine cellar. The London Chop House closed in 1991, but the Caucus Club is still open.

Topinka's Country House was located at 24010 West Seven Mile Road at Telegraph Road. The phone was Kenwood 1-9000. It was the old Sea Food Grotto restaurant with a new addition added. It was open seven days a week and had valet parking. This was the place to go for special occasions like graduations and anniversaries. Santa and his reindeers were always on the roof

of the restaurant during the holiday season. The restaurant was famous for prime rib and turtle soup. It also served family-style chicken dinners on Sundays. The restaurant closed in 1989, was torn down in 1990, and was replaced by a strip mall.

Ken Nicholson owned two Topinkas restaurants in Detroit. This is the Topinkas at 2960 West Grand Boulevard across the street from the Fisher Building. The restaurant was often referred to as "Topinka's town house," and the back of this 1950s postcard says it was "famous from coast to coast."

Galligan's was located at 519 East Jefferson Avenue at Beaubien Street near the Renaissance Center. It opened in 1980 and offered rooftop dining and great views of the Grand Prix races on the streets of Detroit in 1982. By 1992, business had fallen off substantially and the restaurant closed.

Three

METROPOLITAN
DETROIT'S HOTELS
AND RESTAURANTS

The metropolitan Detroit area had many hotels, motels, and restaurants. Included here are a sampling of some early hotels and motels in St. Clair Flats, St. Clair County; Mount Clemens, also called Bath City, USA; Windsor, Ontario, Canada; Plymouth; Farmington; Royal Oak; and, lastly, Dearborn, which is the home of the Ford Motor Company. Dearborn is also the home of the Henry Ford Museum and Greenfield Village that are now part of a larger complex collectively called the Henry Ford. The restaurants shown are in Royal Oak, Grosse Pointe, Livonia, and Mount Clemens.

Joe Bedores Hotel, St. Claire Flats.   Detroit Mich.

Hoping you are in good health I am.
yours Truly II 8 II

Joe Bedore's Hotel, in the St. Clair Flats, was a resort hotel built around 1890. The St. Clair Flats are a series of small islands accessible mainly by boat in the delta waters between Lake St. Clair and the St. Clair River. Although the postcard says "Detroit, Mich." the Flats are actually in St. Clair County. Many Detroit-area residents spent summer vacations in the Flats to escape the heat of the city. This postcard was postmarked in 1906 and was sent to Emma Smith at 293 Greenwood Avenue.

Riverside Hotel, St. Clair Flats, Mich.

Another hotel in the St. Clair Flats was the Riverside Hotel. It was built in 1897 and was more upscale than Joe Bedore's Hotel. Guests could play croquet on the vast lawns and watch Great Lakes vessels thread their way through the narrow channels. The most famous of these ships was the SS *Tashmoo*, which made 10 stops in an hour at this popular resort area.

Another resort area was Mount Clemens in Macomb County, which featured mineral baths that drew people from all over the country. Mount Clemens is about 20 miles from Detroit and billed itself as Bath City, USA. Pictured here is the Park Hotel and park. This lavish and expensive hotel was located at 61 East Street (now North River Road). The hotel and bathhouse were housed in the same building eliminating the necessity of going outside in inclement weather. Many famous people stayed there including Henry Ford, George M. Cohan, Mae West, William Randolph Hearst, and William Jennings Bryan. In 1911, the owners purchased the land across the street that had been occupied by the Avery Hotel, which had burned down. They turned it into a park for the guests of the hotel complete with fountains and beautiful gardens. Business fell off during the Great Depression and dwindled afterwards. By 1937, the hotel was listed as vacant, and it was torn down in 1940.

The Medea Bath House was built in 1882, the second bathhouse to be built in Mount Clemens. It had 150 porcelain tubs making it one of the largest bathhouses in the world, and it was a large-scale operation capable of giving 1,500 baths a day. The rooms were tiled with Italian white marble. The Medea Hotel opened in 1904. The four-story hotel was designed by Theophilus Van Damme. It was especially noted for the 10 massive arches that lined an arcade on Gratiot Avenue. It had 135 nicely appointed guest rooms, which included mahogany furniture, brass bedsteads, and velvet or Wilton carpets. There were also writing rooms, a lady's waiting room, and a buffet and grill in a detached building. The hotel and baths were family-owned by the Ullrich family until 1955. Baths were still given in the bathhouse until 1963, and the building was torn down in 1991. The Mount Clemens Historical Commission sold 300 bricks from the building to collectors.

This advertising postcard from the Business Men's Association of Mount Clemens is of the Elkin Hotel at 37 South Gratiot Avenue from around 1910. The back of the card said the hotel was open all year, located 20 miles from Detroit, and that is was "world renowned for rheumatism, nervousness and that run-down condition." It was owned by Samuel Elkin, a Russian Jew, who came to Mount Clemens about 1907 as a visitor in a wheelchair. He stayed and started a small boardinghouse, then opened the Elkin Hotel to which he added a third story. He also bought the nearby Rudolph Hotel and later the Olympia Hotel. He died in 1929.

This is the beautiful Olympia Hotel and Bath House in Mount Clemens that opened in June 1903. It was located on Cass Avenue next to the Fenton Hotel. It was owned by Charles H. Parsons and Thomas B. Matthews. Among its amenities was a Japanese tearoom. It was purchased by the Elkin family in 1925, who were the owners of the Elkin Hotel. The Elkin family included father Samuel and sons Max and Joseph. The hotel was bought by the City of Mount Clemens in 1955, torn down, and made into a parking lot.

Five women are posed in front of the Hotel Glenwood, which was situated near the Olympia Bath House. It was a small, 40-room hotel and boardinghouse on Cass Avenue that opened in 1900 and was run by Jeannette Reid. There was a Master Humphrey's clock brought over from England in the lobby. The building was razed in January 1975.

Another hotel in Mount Clemens that was connected to a bathhouse was the Monroe Hotel and Plaza Baths, both shown here on this postcard postmarked in 1913. The writer of this card, a person named Sweeney, wrote, "Believe I have got water on the brain." In 1908, the owners were Herman Miller and sons Fred W. and Joseph H. who added the Plaza Hotel in 1912.

The Prince Edward Hotel was located in Windsor, Ontario, Canada, just across the river from Detroit. It is shown here in the 1930s. The Ambassador Bridge, linking the United States with Canada, opened on Veteran's Day in 1929 and the Detroit and Canada Tunnel linking downtown Detroit and Windsor opened the following year. Detroit is actually north of Windsor, so this is a view from Ouellette Avenue in Windsor looking north toward Detroit.

Tunnel Plaza, Windsor, Canada.—119

Here is another view of the Prince Edward Hotel at the tunnel plaza in Windsor in the 1930s. The hotel opened in 1922 and the steel work was erected by the Canadian Bridge Company. It was owned and operated by the United Hotels Company, and it closed July 31, 1967.

Another popular tourist destination is Dearborn. Henry Ford, founder of the Ford Motor Company, opened Greenfield Village and the Henry Ford Museum there in 1929. The Dearborn Inn opened in 1931 to provide rooms for guests visiting these attractions as well as for people doing business with the Ford Motor Company. It was the world's first airport hotel as the Ford airport was across the street on Oakwood Boulevard where the Ford Motor Company test tracks are now located. The guest quarters along Pilots Row originally were used by the airlines' crews. The 179-room Georgian-style hotel was designed by the renowned Albert Kahn and featured a ballroom with a high ceiling and crystal chandeliers. It was managed by the L.G. Treadway Service of New York. The hotel has two Michigan historic markers and was placed on the National Register of Historic Places in 1990.

Shown here is the lobby of the Dearborn Inn in the 1940s on an unused black-and-white postcard. Hotel guests could relax here in front of a cozy fire after a busy day. Some of the famous people who stayed here were Orville Wright, Jack Dempsey, Eleanor Roosevelt, Bob Hope, Norman Rockwell, and Duncan Hines. Hines wrote in the guest book, "This is my favorite Inn."

The Old English Coffee Shop of the Dearborn Inn is shown on another black-and-white unused postcard from the 1950s. The knotty pine walls and Early American furniture gave it a homey atmosphere. The coffee shop later became the Ten Eyck Tavern that is still used for casual dining.

This 1960s-era postcard is of the McGuffey Building of the Motor House at the Dearborn Inn. This building and the Burbank building comprised the Motor House section of the inn's 185 rooms. All the rooms in the Motor House were furnished with reproductions of fabrics and furniture from the Henry Ford Museum and Greenfield Village that was located across the street. Other amenities included a heated pool, putting green, tennis courts, children's playground, two restaurants, and a cocktail lounge. The McGuffey Building was named after William McGuffey who developed the first readers for primary schools, and the Burbank building was named after Luther Burbank who was a botanist and a pioneer in agricultural science.

A typical guest room in the Dearborn Inn in the 1960s was a king-sized, canopied bed and 19th century–style reproduction furniture. All the reproductions were based on furniture in the collections of the Henry Ford Museum and Greenfield Village. There were also 23 acres of beautifully landscaped grounds for guests to enjoy.

In 1937, the Dearborn Inn's accommodations were expanded with replicas of historically famous homes. Here are three of the five Colonial homes that were used to provide additional accommodations for guests of the Dearborn Inn. They are the original Walt Whitman house from Melville, Long Island; the Edgar Allen Poe cottage from Fordham in New York City; and the Barbara Fritchie House from Frederick, Maryland. Each building is an exact exterior reproduction of its namesake's house while the interiors were modified to provide hotel accommodations. They are still in use today as hotel guest rooms.

The Barbara Fritchie House is shown on this 1930s postcard as it looked when it was new. It is a one-and-a-half-story brick cottage. Fritchie was a patriot, and it is said that she waved the Union flag out of her window while Stonewall Jackson's troops were passing through Frederick in the Maryland campaign. She was 95 at the time and died a year later at the age of 96.

The Walt Whitman House is shown on this 1930s postcard as it looked when it was new. The original was a two-story, brick, federal-style building that was built by his father, a house builder, on Long Island, New York, in 1816. It is still standing and is on the National Register of Historic Places. Whitman was a poet and famous for his *Leaves of Grass*, which is considered a literary masterpiece.

The Edgar Allen Poe House is shown new on this 1930s postcard. The original was a small, one-and-a-half-story cottage in Fordham, New York, which was built in 1812. Poe leased the home for $100 per year. Although Poe was an author, editor, and the inventor of the mystery novel, he died penniless.

The Patrick Henry House is a large, two-story, frame federal-style building with symmetrical flanking wings. Patrick Henry was a Revolutionary War patriot, famous for saying, "give me liberty or give me death." This house, as well as all the other Colonial Village homes, was furnished with antique reproduction furniture.

This is the Dearborn Inn as it looked in the early 1960s. At the time, it was nestled among stately elm trees that are now long gone. This postcard advertises that it was the world's first airport hotel and had been built by Henry Ford. It had 185 guest rooms at that time and now has 222 rooms and suites. It has also since been expanded to include 17,000 square feet of event space for meetings, banquets, weddings, and so on. It is now a part of the Marriott Hotel chain.

HOTEL DEARBORN ON MICHIGAN AVE. — DEARBORN, MICH.

Dearborn was also the home of the Hotel Dearborn, which was located at 4616 Calhoun Street at Michigan Avenue. The phone number in 1941 was Oregon 2500. The hotel advertised that it was homelike and comfortable and convenient to all points of interest. They had rooms with or without baths and rates starting at $1.50 a day; there were also special weekly rates. The hotel had a coffee shop. In 1941, J. H. Gustav Steffens was the manager there. The building was razed in February 1979.

HOTEL FORDSON
DEARBORN, MICH.

U. S. 112
MICHIGAN
AND
JONATHAN AVENUES
NEAR
SCHAEFER ROAD

The Hotel Fordson was another Dearborn hotel managed by J. H. Gustav Steffens. It is located at 4818 Jonathon Street. They advertised that they were on the "edge of Detroit" and "nearest to the Ford Motor Company Plant Offices and Rotunda Building." The Rotunda Building was a major Dearborn attraction that burned down in 1962. It was a 12-story structure with a circular exterior built for the Chicago World's Fair in 1933 and 1934 and taken down after the fair and rebuilt in Dearborn in 1936. By the 1950s, the Rotunda was the fifth major tourist destination in the United States. It was more popular than Yellowstone Park or the Statue of Liberty and featured a Christmas fantasy display with a 37-foot, six-ton Christmas tree. Nearly 500,000 people visited the Rotunda the first year of the Christmas display, and it is estimated that about six million people visited the display in the nine years the Christmas fantasy was held. This hotel is still in business. It has been renovated and is now part of the America's Best Value Inn chain.

DEARBORN TOURIST COURT
2 Blocks West of U. S. 24 on U. S. 112
Dearborn, Michigan

The Dearborn Tourist Court was an early Dearborn motel located at 24623 Michigan Avenue two blocks west of Telegraph Road (U.S. Route 24). Hugh J. Callahan was listed as the manager on the back of this 1950s postcard. Hugh C. McDonald, the name of the previous owner, was scratched out. This motel became rundown, was boarded up, and it was torn down in the 1990s.

Moore's Motel (New Colonial Brick) 25125 Michigan Avenue, Dearborn.
Phone Lo. 2-9757 - Open All Year

Moore's Motel (New Colonial Brick) was located at 25125 Michigan Avenue in Dearborn. It was a half-mile west of Telegraph Road (U.S. Route 24) and seven miles from the Detroit city limits. It was owned and managed by Mr. and Mrs. Homer Moore. The phone number was Logan 2-9757.

The Dearborn Towne House Motel was located at 2101 South Telegraph Road (U.S. Route 24) at Michigan Avenue. It advertised 101 luxurious, air conditioned rooms, a cocktail lounge, a dining room, and heated pool on this 1960s postcard. It was owned by Harry Chrysan who also owned a car wash in Dearborn.

Jean's Dearborn Motor Lodge was located at 2211 South Telegraph Road, two blocks south of Michigan Avenue. It advertised that it was AAA approved, air conditioned with radiant heat, near Greenfield Village, and had color television. It opened about 1958 and was owned by Russell J. Comer and Marjorie G. Wessels.

The Holiday Inn was located at 22900 Michigan Avenue near Outer Drive in Dearborn and was a Dearborn landmark for many years. It was part of a nationwide chain that was founded by Kemmons Wilson in 1952. The motels were named after the Bing Crosby movie of the same name. This one opened November 12, 1964, on the site of the old St. Joseph's Retreat that closed in 1962 and was torn down in 1963. This Holiday Inn had over 300 rooms, a swimming pool, wading pool, children's playground, a dining room, coffee shop, and a cocktail lounge. It is shown here on this 5¢ postcard at its peak in the late 1960s. It housed the Chambertin, which was one of Dearborn's best restaurants. The motel was razed to make way for a Farmer Jack supermarket.

The Westerner Beef Buffet shown here on a 1960s advertising postcard was located at 24825 Michigan Avenue, one quarter mile west of Telegraph Road. It advertised itself as a "real family style restaurant," and invited people to "come as you are." It was open seven days a week. The food was served cafeteria style. Their roast beef sandwich on an onion roll could not be beat.

Baja's billed itself as "Dearborn's finest cocktail lounge and dining room" in the 1960s. It was located on Michigan Avenue at the corner of Telegraph Road. It was owned by John Baja Jr. The menu featured fresh live lobsters, seafood, and charcoal broiled steaks. A hot and cold buffet smorgasbord was served every Tuesday evening. The building was torn down and was replaced by an E-Z storage facility.

The Mayflower Hotel billed itself as a 100-room historic bed-and-breakfast hotel. A full complimentary breakfast was included for overnight guests. Deluxe rooms featured Kohler whirlpool bathtubs and king-sized beds. The three-story hotel opened in the late 1920s and was located at 827 Ann Arbor Trail at Main Street in Plymouth. It advertised that it was minutes away from the Detroit Metropolitan Airport, Ann Arbor, Detroit, and Greenfield Village, and within walking distance of 150 unique shops, tree-lined Kellogg Park, and a movie theater. The banquet facilities could serve 400, and it had six meeting rooms. It was family-operated and was known for its Sunday brunch. The hotel was torn down in September 1999, and it was replaced with high-end condominiums with retail space on the street level.

Reproductions of paintings that hang in Pilgrim Hall in Plymouth, Massachusetts, used to hang in the walls of the dining room of the Mayflower Hotel. There were nine, full-color paintings depicting the life of the pilgrims that were done by various artists. *The Return of the Mayflower* was painted by George Boughton.

The art deco–style Oakotel Hotel Café and Terraces is shown here on this 1940s black-and-white postcard. The sign in the front of the hotel says it is a tourist hotel. Inside were modern, furnished apartments and sleeping rooms. The hotel was located about 15 miles from Detroit on M-10 in Royal Oak, and was a half-mile north of the Shrine of the Little Flower and near the Detroit Zoological Park.

HEDGE'S WIGWAM, WOODWARD AVE. AT 10 MILE RD., ROYAL OAK, MICH.

Hedge's Wigwam was a well-known table service dining room on Woodward Avenue at Twelve Mile Road in Royal Oak, a northern suburb of Detroit. It was a very popular restaurant with a Native American motif. It operated in conjunction with a cafeteria that was at Woodward Avenue and Ten Mile Road, and it also had a gift shop. It burned down about 1970. One of the four wooden Indians in front of Hedge's Wigwam later found its way to the front of the Paint Creek Cider Mill in Rochester.

HEDGE'S WIGWAM   DETROIT, MICHIGAN

This is the interior of Hedge's Wigwam. It was known for excellent food, especially the barbecued beef sandwiches and chicken pot pies that were recommended by Duncan Hines. It was one of the stops for the teenagers who cruised Woodward Avenue in the 1950s and 1960s before the days of the Woodward Dream Cruise.

HEDGE'S WIGWAM   DETROIT, MICHIGAN

Another view of the interior of Hedge's Wigwam shows the unusual rustic décor. Moose heads were mounted on the walls. Both Hedge's Wigwam and the cafeteria restaurant were near the Shrine of the Little Flower and the Detroit Zoological Park, which were popular destinations for both residents and tourists.

The Grand Tulane Motel was located on Grand River Avenue at Middlebelt Road in Farmington, a western suburb of Detroit. The phone was Greenleaf 4-9880. It advertised modern furnishings, carpeting, tile showers, free television, and a restaurant adjacent to the motel. It was owned and managed by Mr. and Mrs. E. Sierens.

Shown here is Stouffer's restaurant, which was located in the Eastland Shopping Center in Harper Woods. There were four dining rooms including the Victorian Room, which was decorated like the Gaslight Era, and the Pointe Room, which was a banquet room for parties, weddings, and meetings. The original Detroit Stouffer's opened on Clifford Street in 1929, and Stouffer's was one of the nation's largest restaurant chains in the 1960s.

The Cranbrook House was located on James Couzens Highway and had a Detroit mailing address. It was adjacent to the Northland Shopping Mall in Southfield that opened in 1954 and was the area's first major shopping mall. The anchor store was J. L. Hudson's, which later became Marshall Field, and is currently Macy's.

The Village Manor was a large dining establishment at 685 St. Clair Street near Kercheval Street in Grosse Pointe. The phone was Tuxedo 2-1110. It was owned by Richard and Florence Lehman. Shown on this color postcard are the lobby and food shop, the Williamsburg Room, and the St. Clair Room.

Moy's in Livonia offered Chinese dining along with a 100-year-old Chinese statue of "Quon Yen," which signified the Goddess of Mercy. The statue was completely carved out of camphor wood. The restaurant was located at 16825 Middlebelt Road.

This advertising postcard is for Gino's Surf on 37400 Jefferson Avenue on Lake St. Clair between Fifteen Mile Road and Metropolitan Parkway. This large restaurant has views of the lake from the main dining room and has a Sunday brunch with a large assortment of food. It also has banquet rooms and caters to weddings, office parties, and business luncheons.

ACROSS AMERICA, PEOPLE ARE DISCOVERING SOMETHING WONDERFUL. *THEIR HERITAGE.*

Arcadia Publishing is the leading local history publisher in the United States. With more than 3,000 titles in print and hundreds of new titles released every year, Arcadia has extensive specialized experience chronicling the history of communities and celebrating America's hidden stories, bringing to life the people, places, and events from the past. To discover the history of other communities across the nation, please visit:

www.arcadiapublishing.com

Customized search tools allow you to find regional history books about the town where you grew up, the cities where your friends and family live, the town where your parents met, or even that retirement spot you've been dreaming about.